Are Ghosts Real?

BY PATRICK PERISH

amicus
high interest

Amicus High Interest is published by Amicus
P.O. Box 1329, Mankato, MN 56002
www.amicuspublishing.us

Library of Congress Cataloging-in-Publication Data
Perish, Patrick.
 Are ghosts real? / Patrick Perish.
    p. cm. -- (Unexplained, what's the evidence?)
 Includes index.
   ISBN 978-1-60753-384-9 (library binding) -- ISBN 978-1-
60753-432-7 (ebook)
1. Ghosts--Juvenile literature. I. Title.
 BF1461.P435 2014
 133.1--dc23
                                    2012036392

Editor   Rebecca Glaser
Series Designer   Kathleen Petelinsek
Page production   Red Line Editorial, Inc.

Photo Credits
Dreamstime, cover; iStockphoto, 5; Esteban De Armas/
Shutterstock Images, 6; Library of Congress, 9, 23; Mark
Humphrey/AP Images, 10; Charles Temple Dix/Public
Domain, 13; Shelli Jensen/Shutterstock Images, 15; Yu Lan/
Shutterstock Images, 16; Shutterstock Images, 19; Morry
Gash/AP Images, 20; 123RF, 24; Thinkstock, 27; Sandra
Cunningham/Shutterstock Images, 29

Printed in the United States of America at Corporate Graphics
in North Mankato, Minnesota.
5-2013 / P.O. 1152
10 9 8 7 6 5 4 3 2 1

Table of Contents

What Are Ghosts?   4

Old Ghost Stories   11

Recent Ghost Stories   17

Exposing the Fakes   22

What's the Evidence?   26

Glossary   30

Read More   31

Websites   31

Index   32

What Are Ghosts?

Around the world people tell ghost stories. Some tell about doors that open by themselves. Some tell about strange noises in the night. Some even tell about people who appear out of nowhere. Are these just stories? Or are they something more?

Many people like to tell ghost stories around a campfire.

Are ghosts real? All we have are stories.

Q What kinds of ghosts are reported?

What are ghosts? Some say they are evil. Many say they are spirits of the dead. No one is sure where ghosts come from. Some think ghosts are only in people's minds. Others think ghosts are part of the unseen world. There is no hard proof for ghosts, only stories.

 All kinds! Some are **invisible**. Some are animals. Some seem to be stuck in time. Others try to get a message to the living.

Some ghosts are like **recordings**. They do the same thing over and over. Many ghosts have been seen at old battlefields. In Gettysburg, Pennsylvania, people have seen ghosts of soldiers. One ghost looks like he's climbing a wall. But there is no wall there! These ghosts can't see people. They are stuck in time.

 Who looks for ghosts?

The Battle of Gettysburg took place in 1863 during the Civil War.

 People called ghost hunters look for ghosts. Some are on TV. Ghost hunting is their job. They have lots of equipment. Others do it just for fun.

Carney Bell is a descendant of the haunted Bell family.

3C   38

BELL WITCH

he north was the farm of John Bell, early, prominent settler from North olina. According to legend, his family harried during the early 19th century the famous Bell Witch. She kept the house d in turmoil, assaulted Bell, and dro f Betsy Bell's suitor. Even Andrew Jac ho came to investigate, retreated to fter his coach wheels stopped Many visitors to the house saw the crash, about them, and heard h sing, and curse.

Old Ghost Stories

A Tennessee family was haunted in the early 1800s. The Bells were rich farmers. One summer, weird things started happening. They saw strange birds and dogs in the field. Then, the animals disappeared. The Bells heard lots of banging under their floor. At night, their blankets were pulled off. After the father died, the ghost left.

Some ghosts aren't people. Some people have seen ghost trains, trucks, and even ships. The most famous ghost ship is the Flying Dutchman. Legends say the crew is doomed to sail forever. Seeing it is a bad **omen**. It brings bad luck. In 1939, people in South Africa saw a spooky ship sail through the bay and disappear. Was it the Flying Dutchman?

 How do scientists explain ghost ships?

Charles Temple Dix painted this picture of the Flying Dutchman.

 Scientists think most ghost ships are caused by **mirages**. A mirage is a trick of the light. It makes strange shapes appear.

Some ghosts appear to people when they die. Gladys Watson lived in Indiana. One night, she heard her name. She woke up. Her grandpa was standing over her bed. He told her not to be scared. Then he disappeared! She called her parents. They were already awake. They had just heard the news. Her grandpa had died.

Some say they have seen ghosts of family members.

Some people think ghosts can make a big mess.

 What is a poltergeist?

Recent Ghost Stories

In 1967 in Germany, strange things happened at a law office. Pictures and cabinets moved on their own. Lights went off all at once. Phones rang when no one was calling. It seemed like a **poltergeist**. Many experts checked the office. But no one could find a cause. After a secretary stopped working there, the poltergeist stopped.

 Poltergeist is a German word. It means "noisy ghost." A poltergeist likes to throw and break things. Usually, it can't be seen.

Many people report seeing a ghost **hitchhiker**. Here is one story from Chicago. A man was driving home at night. It was raining. He saw a girl on the side of the road. The man picked her up. When he drove past the graveyard, she vanished! Some say she died in a car accident years ago. More than 30 people have reported this ghost.

Tales of hitchhiking ghosts have been popular throughout history.

Even some athletes are scared of ghosts. The Pfister Hotel is in Milwaukee. It was built in 1893. Many sports teams stay there for away games. Weird noises are heard at night. A Cardinals player saw floating lights in his room. One of the Dodgers even sleeps with a baseball bat for safety!

Many famous people have stayed at the Pfister Hotel.

Exposing the Fakes

Some people make up ghost stories. They want attention or money. In 1848, two girls in New York fooled everyone. Margaret and Kate Fox heard tapping. It was a ghost, they said. They asked it questions. One tap meant "no." Three taps meant "yes." They became famous. When they were old, they said they had faked the ghost. They made the noises by snapping their toes!

Kate (left) and Margaret Fox (right) pose with their older sister Leah.

In 2008, a ghost was caught on video. The video showed two men in an elevator. They rode it up. It stopped. When they got out, the ghost of an old woman appeared. Later, a company said they made the video. They made it to show people the dangers of working late.

Ghost stories can be made up to entertain us or trick us.

What's the Evidence?

There are many ideas about ghosts. Some think chemicals in the brain make people see strange things. Others think ghost sightings are caused by energy waves. And some people still think ghosts really are dead spirits. Ghost hunters keep looking. They hope to find proof.

 How do ghost hunters look for ghosts?

People looking for ghosts might try to catch them on video.

 Some ghost hunters use special machines. They measure the energy in a room. If the reading is high, it might mean ghosts are nearby.

Most proof for ghosts comes from stories. Some photos and videos can't be explained. But they don't prove ghosts are real. Photos and videos can be faked. Some ghost stories can't be explained. And they are told around the world. But ghosts are still a mystery. Maybe someday scientists will solve it. What do you think?

 How many people believe in ghosts?

A house on a hill is a common setting for a ghost story.

A 2005 poll showed almost one-third of Americans believe in ghosts.

Glossary

hitchhiker Someone who gets a ride from someone else, usually a stranger.

invisible Unable to be seen.

mirage A trick of the light that makes people see things that aren't there.

omen A sign of future good or evil.

poltergeist An invisible ghost that breaks things.

recordings Something that can be played over and over.

Read More

Bouvier, Charles. *The Ghost Hunter's Guide.* Monster Tracker. Mankato, Minn.: Sea-to-Sea Publications, 2012.

Martin, Michael. *Ghost Hunters.* Ghost Files. Mankato, Minn.: Capstone Press, 2012.

Stone, Adam. *Ghosts.* The Unexplained. Minneapolis: Bellwether Media, 2011.

Websites

Discovery Kids
http://kids.discovery.com/games/skill/zap-a-ghost

Ghost Hunting for Kids
http://kids.ghostvillage.com/

Snopes – Lifting Spirits, the Raffles Place Ghost
http://www.snopes.com/photos/supernatural/elevatorghost.asp

Index

Bell family 11

energy 26-27

fake ghosts 22, 25

Flying Dutchman 12

Fox, Margaret and Kate 22

Germany 17

Gettysburg 8

ghost hitchhiker 18

ghost hunters 9, 26-27

ghost ships 12-13

mirages 13

Pfister Hotel 21

poltergeists 16-17

proof 7, 26, 28

recordings 8

spirits 7, 26

types of ghosts 7

video 25, 28

Watson, Gladys 14

About the Author

Patrick Perish spent many childhood nights under the covers with a flashlight and good book. In particular, aliens, ghosts, and other unexplained mysteries have always kept him up until the wee hours of the night. He lives in Minneapolis, MN where he writes and edits children's books.